BUILDING A MARRIAGE CULTURE

RENEWAL IN THE RUINS

Editors: Grant Castleberry
and Greg Gibson

Series Editor: Owen Strachan

CBMW PRESS

Copyright ©2015 by CBMW

All rights reserved. No part of this publication may be reproduced in any form without written permission from the author. Made and designed in the United States of America.

ISBN-13: 978-0692524077
ISBN-10: 069252407X

Scripture quotations are from The Holy Bible, English Standard Version® (ESV®), copyright © 2001 by Crossway, a publishing ministry of Good News Publishers. Used by permission. All rights reserved.

Cover Design by Landon Reynolds

Layout & Design by Mathew B. Sims

www.MathewBryanSims.com

To Wayne and Margaret Grudem, who have lived, modeled, and taught God's great design for marriage.

TABLE OF CONTENT

Introduction — 9
Greg Gibson

Part 1: Rebuilding in the Ruins — 12

1 Husbands, Love Your Wives — 13
Gavin Peacock

2 Fathers, Love Your Children — 19
Grant Castleberry

3 Pastors, Teach Your People — 24
Owen Strachan

4 Husbands, Honor Your Wives — 29
Greg Gibson

5 Wives, Serve Your Husbands — 34
Courtney Reissig

6 Women, Esteem Godly Men — 38
Amanda Peacock

7 Mothers, Love Your Children — 43
GraceAnna Castleberry

8 Women, Own Your Identity — 47
Candi Finch

Part 2: Responding to the SCOTUS Decision — 52

9 Official Response to the SCOTUS Ruling
CBMW Staff & Board — 53

10 The Supreme Court Has Ruled: What Should Christians Do?
Owen Strachan — 58

11 Parenting in a Gay Marriage World: What Should Christian Parents Do?
Greg Gibson — 64

About the Authors — 71

INTRODUCTION
Greg Gibson

It is no secret that biblical marriage is under attack today. Over the past couple of decades, culture has fought to redefine marriage as something besides one woman and one man. Recently, the Supreme Court has done just that—redefining marriage to include same-sex marriage.

It is more pressing than ever that Christians—and local churches—stand firm on marriage.

At CBMW, we stand on the conviction of God's authoritative Word. We believe the Bible. We believe it is without error. We believe God's Word is the foundation of all meaning, direction, and joy in our lives. Furthermore, we believe God created the institution of marriage (Gen. 2:18-25). He placed Adam and Eve in the Garden of Eden to enjoy one another to the fullest. There was no brokenness, corruption, adultery, abandonment, immorality, money problems, in-law drama, or all the other effects of sin that creep into a marriage. And there were no attempts at a new definition of marriage either.

The results of sin on our world are vast. Within the framework of marriage, sin abounds. The Lord Jesus Christ ultimately redeems marriage by redeeming broken people. Dave Harvey says it best, "Until sin be bitter, marriage will not be sweet."[1] Within culture, there is no moral compass guiding marriage. Much like everything in our atheological and postmodern culture, marriage has lost objective meaning, being redefined in the eyes of the definer—who, as it seems, is anyone and everyone.

The Bible defines marriage as a reflection of Christ and His Bride—a mystery that points to the sacrificial relationship between Jesus and the Church (Eph. 5). It is to be between one man and one woman. We are going to stand firm on that truth, because logically, if you redefine marriage, you begin to redefine the gospel.

With all that said, in a world where same-sex marriage is now legal in all 50 states, how should men, women, and churches continue to stand firm on marriage? We stand firm by pursuing our God-given spouse, endlessly loving our children in a biblical way, and by rebuilding a marriage culture—Nehemiah style—that glorifies the Lord Jesus Christ and is in turn used for our great good.

It is that simple.

---

[1] Dave Harvey, *When Sinners Say "I Do,"* (Wapwallopen, PA: Shepherd Press, 2010).

Introduction

Marriage is good. It is beautiful. It is holy. Let us recommit to it, and rebuild in the ruins.

We will stand firm on marriage no matter the cost. It is our hope that this book will equip you to stand faithfully for marriage—in Christ alone—against the cultural tide of this new definition. We believe this book will not only equip you to stand strong, but it will equip you to stand strong with a joy unstoppable, because God's design for marriage is that good.

PART 1
REBUILDING IN THE RUINS

1
HUSBANDS, LOVE YOUR WIVES

Gavin Peacock

Despite Friday's SCOTUS decision, the Bible's view of marriage remains unchanged—one man and one woman, displaying the gospel for life (Gen. 2:24; Eph. 5). How should the church respond? We must show that biblical marriage is not only right, but also it is good, and then we must out-rejoice the opposition. The church is called to be holy, so we must build a marriage culture that reflects God's holy character.

Therefore, the first call is this: "Husbands, love your wives." The husband is the head of his wife, because he is male. However, the characteristic of *love* is his special duty toward her and defines his leadership.

Husbands, here are three masculine exhortations:

LOVE YOUR WIFE BECAUSE GOD COMMANDS IT

This is your foundation. God wills that you love her as he has loved you (Eph. 5:25). Your security is in God's love for you, and it is what propels this kind of love towards your wife. She won't always respond well to your initiatives in the home and attempts to lead her and the family. She might push back at times.

But you must be like Christ when he kneeled to wash Peter's feet (John 13). Peter, part of the Bride of Christ, refused this loving leadership, but Jesus didn't get discouraged and give up. He stayed at Peter's feet and told Peter this must be done for his good. Men, we don't have time for self-pity and passivity. We must humble ourselves, absorb injustice, and persevere. A loving leadership of your wife isn't contingent on her response or your feelings, but on God's will: "Husbands, love your wives!"

LOVE YOUR WIFE IN ALL WAYS, FOR ALWAYS, AND ABOVE ALL OTHERS

- **Love her in all ways:** Love her by being her physical protector. Christ protects the church, not the other way around. A husband is no man if he lets his wife defend the home or sends his wife to defend the country.

  Love her by being her physical lover. Your body is not your own. You are

Husbands, Love Your Wives

obligated to use it firstly for her pleasure, not your own selfish gain (1 Cor. 7:3).

Love her through your physical provision. Work hard and aim to to be the main breadwinner. There may be a temporary season, if you're studying or in transition, where that is not so. Or you may be physically disabled, which prevents this permanently. But the desire and aim should still be there.

Love her through your spiritual leadership. This is where most men struggle or abdicate, because this takes time and spiritual sweat. A husband's love for his wife means he is more concerned for her holiness than for his comfort. What is more, in your personal devotions mine for gold, not just for yourself but also for her, so you can sanctify your wife with the Word (Eph. 5:26). Don't drown her with an hour-long doctrinal dissertation. Give her a biblical nugget and make application to her life as you live with her in an understanding way, knowing her needs almost before she asks (1 Peter 3:7).

- **Love her for always:** Your commitment to her is permanent because Christ's commitment to his Bride is permanent. You are one flesh. Love her as you do your own body, always aware of her, always keeping her warm, and always seeking her good (Eph. 5:29). Some men pray for God to fix their wife's problems while they do nothing, but her problems are your problems. You are her permanent head, not part-time head. Go towards her and be her main human means of sanctification. Is she growing in godliness directly because of your consistent loving leadership?

- **Love her above all others:** Cherish her (Eph. 5:29)! Love her with a laser focus, so she will feel cherished. Satisfy yourself with her alone (Prov. 5:19). Date her and woo her. Place her above the children in your affections, and with your attention, because you are one flesh with her, not them. They will feel most loved when they see the way their father loves their mother with special covenant love.

    Encourage her when you see her growing in godly femininity. Praise her inner *and* outer beauty. She needs to know you find her physically attractive, as well as spiritually attractive. Comfort her when she is hurting and listen to her when you want the bullet points of the story and she wants to give fine detail. In all these things, you are communicating that you cherish her above all others.

Husbands, Love Your Wives

LOVE YOUR WIFE WITH MANLY AUTHORITY AND MANLY

Make decisions, but discuss all things with her. She is your greatest counselor, equal to you, but created by God for you to lead. Her wisdom is priceless, as she knows you better than anyone else. However, if a decision must be made and you are both in deadlock, then you are responsible before God to make that decision. If it goes well, don't gloat over her; if it goes wrong, protect her from the fall-out.

Delegate authority to your wife, but remember she needs to see that you are her authority. Be a holy man of the Word and prayer. Not effeminate, but masculine. Not rash and foolish, but patient and wise. Your leadership, then, won't be self-willed. It will be spiritually empowered, and it will encourage her reverence. Your headship is God's design for her protection and growth. If you don't assume the manly mantle, then she is left exposed and vulnerable to attack and her femininity will be compromised.

Yet manly authority must be paired with manly tenderness. Be firm with your wife, but never harsh (Col. 3:19). If she is tired and worried, speak tender words from Scripture to comfort her. If you are in conflict with her, take the log out your own eye first. This has the effect of tenderizing your own soul, as you once again appropriate the gospel and the perfect patience and tender mercies of Christ to you.

Building a Marriage Culture

Marriage is not socially defined but divinely designed. Therefore, it's true meaning will stand when society crumbles (Rev. 19:9). And a marriage where a husband loves his wife like this is a little bit of heaven on earth.

2
FATHERS, LOVE YOUR CHILDREN
Grant Castleberry

By buying into the homosexual movement, the culture has implicitly said that the uniqueness of fatherhood and motherhood does not really matter. The Bible, however, places maximum value on both a father and a mother in a child's life.

Let's zero in on the Christian view of fatherhood as we seek to rebuild a marriage culture in the ruins.

THE FOUNDATION OF FATHERHOOD

God cares immensely about fatherhood in the family. When I lost my own father when I was two years old, my mom comforted me with the fact that God promises to be a "father to the fatherless" (Psalm 68:5). God places a premium on fatherhood to the extent that he promises to be a father to fatherless covenant children. In the New Testament, Jesus teaches us to address God as Father in the Lord's Prayer (Matt 6:9). Because of this revolutionary prayer, Jesus's teaching on the fatherhood of God has been the model for how the Christian church is to relate to God through the centuries.

It is from this truth—*the fatherhood of God*—that the Christian church has constructed its view of fatherhood in the Christian family. It is from the character of our own heavenly Father that Christian fathers have understood how to relate to their children. So as the church embarks into a post-SCOTUS marriage world, it is due time that we double down on fatherhood, taking our cues from our own heavenly Father so that we might point a lost world to Him through our lives.

FATHERS DEMONSTRATE UNCONDITIONAL LOVE

The Christian view of love is unconditional. We know this because of Paul's words in Romans 5:8. "God shows his love for us in that while we were still sinners, Christ died for us," the apostle writes. This means that the love of a Christian father, mirroring the Father's love for His children, must be undaunted and unflinching. Even if the child has vast ideological differences and spurns his own father's love, the Christian father continues to reach out in extraordinary love.

When the great writer Robert Louis Stevenson went off to college at the University of Edinburgh, he renounced the Christian faith. His father, a devout Presbyterian, mourned his son's choice, but never stopped loving his son. Throughout Stevenson's global travels, his father continued to send money to him and prayed regularly for Robert's soul. This continued until he died, though Robert never repented and reconciled his relationship with his father. Sometimes, the prodigal does not come home.

Whether our children respond or not, this type of unconditional, radical love that pursues even when love is not returned will set Christian fathers apart going forward. Fathers, love your own children with the radical, unconditional love that your heavenly Father has shown you. The world does not know that love, but when they see it, they will be beholding the very love of God. What a calling this is.

FATHERS DISCIPLINE THEIR CHILDREN

The Christian worldview recognizes that discipline is good for children. They need it. It teaches them right from wrong and instructs them on how to walk in the path of godliness. That is why our Heavenly Father "disciplines the one he loves, and chastises every son whom he receives."

The writer of Hebrews relates God's discipline of his spiritual children directly to fatherhood when he says, "For what son is there whom his father does not discipline" (Heb 12:7). The Lord disciplines his children because he loves us and wants us to flourish. As a Christian father lovingly takes responsibility for the discipline of his children, he will set them on a trajectory of wisdom in the knowledge of God (Prov 3:12). His children will be trained as beacons of light in a world of confusion because they know the God of order and will "live long in the land."

Fathers: much as the culture pushes against the concept, we must not give up on the faithful, diligent discipline of our children. It is in the loving discipline of our children that we will shape the next generation of Christians before a watching world.

FATHERS DO NOT PROVOKE THEIR CHILDREN TO ANGER

God promises to "work all things together for good" for His children (Rom 8:28). Likewise, the Christian father also should strive to serve his children in every way for their good. Perhaps nothing is more hypocritical than a Christian father who claims to have experienced the love and goodness of God and then turns around and is provoking, wrathful, or disinterested in his children. That is why Paul directly instructs Christian fathers to "not provoke your children to anger, lest they become discouraged" (Col 3:21).

There are a myriad of ways a father could provoke his children, whether it be through neglect, inconsistent discipline, favoritism, living vicariously through his children, making unfair comparisons, or numerous other harmful actions.

A father, as the head of the household, must avoid the pitfalls of sin toward his children that will push his children away from the gospel and the Lord Jesus. We cannot be overbearing, on the one hand; we cannot be disengaged, on the other.

FATHERS PROVIDE SECURITY

The world is a cold, dark place where sin reigns. Yet in the midst of difficulty there is solace to be found in the comforting protection of our Father. The Psalmist writes in Psalm 91 that God will cover his children "with his pinions, and under his wings you will find refuge; his faithfulness is a shield and a buckler" (Ps 91:4). The picture is of a mother bird, who covers her young—protecting them from predators by sacrificing her own body for the lives of her young.

God has already shown us how much he will provide security for us through the death of Christ. And Christ himself promises that no one will be able to take the Christian out of His hand (John 10:28). Likewise, as Christian fathers, we must strive to be the embodiment of security and protection in the life of our children. We can do this not only by working hard to provide physical protection to our children, but by also pointing them to the spiritual security provided to us by our Heavenly father.

In the midst of the trials that await us, we must be strong in the Lord for our children and continually point them to where ultimate security is found: in the shadow of the wings of the Lord.

3
PASTORS, TEACH YOUR PEOPLE
Owen Strachan

Will we be able to build marriage cultures in our churches? If so, we must have pastors who teach their people. Let's zero in on how pastors can honor God and strengthen the flock by preaching the Bible's vision of manhood and womanhood, sexuality, and marriage.

FIRST, PASTORS MUST RECOGNIZE THAT THEY HAVE COMPETITORS

For too long, many Christian pastors have either shied away from hard issues or assumed that people under their leadership will naturally embrace contested biblical truths. We are tempted to think that if we put the right books on the shelves, all the manifold complementarian wisdom of Wayne Grudem and John Piper will somehow waft its way to the minds of church members, magically traveling from book to brain without any action on our part.

In fact, the opposite is true. We have competitors. Many competitors. A secularist culture is quite eager to train our people, and set them straight. We should expect that the hours spent in front of televisions or browsing on iPads will soften their view of divorce, ramp up their sympathy for gay marriage, and increase their appetite for sexual promiscuity. All around us are worldview educators, those skilled in the affecting presentation of sin and its fruits. Pastors are in a great competition for the souls of their people.

This need not drive anyone to fear. It should motivate us to approach ministry with sobriety and great care. Here's the great news: we have a sure authority and a perfect law (Psalm 19:7). We don't need tricks and gimmicks. We simply need to open the Word of God to our people and unleash it on the congregation. It will benevolently conquer the hearts of the children of God. The gospel is undefeated, and it will triumph over its competitors.

SECOND, PASTORS MUST EQUIP PARENTS TO CLEAR THEIR THROATS

There is no group in the church that will more feel the culture's fingers on their pressure-points than parents. Fathers and mothers have an increasingly difficult task in their quest to educate their children in a complementarian worldview, for the culture has removed many of the structural supports for this wise body of thought. Marriage is now make-your-own; gender and sexuality is now what-do-you-feel-like. In such a time, parents must own afresh their God-given responsibility to teach and model what is true (see Proverbs 2; 1 Timothy 3).

If marriage is to be esteemed by the rising generation, fathers and mothers must both teach what marriage is and pursue a God-glorifying union. Teaching without demonstration will leave kids jaded; demonstration without teaching will leave kids uninformed. Marriage is supposed to be a living display of love, even cosmically covenantal love (Eph. 5:22-33). We should not leave our children to marvel, however. We need to talk them through what lifelong union is, even as we discuss why transgenderism is wrong and tragic, and how sexual perversity bound only by consent will destroy the soul. If ever Christian parents have been embarrassed to say these things, we cannot be any more.

Pastors set parents up for success by preaching and teaching on marriage, manhood and womanhood, biblical sexuality, and related topics. When the pulpit is strong on these issues, the elders will know how to handle tough matters, the small-group leaders will be equipped to pray with wisdom, and parents will have a blueprint for training their children. When the pulpit is silent on such matters, and the pastor is quiet as a church mouse because he "wants to be known for what he's for, not against," then the church as a body will languish and parents will struggle to speak.

Pastors: train fathers and mothers to train boys and girls.

THIRD, PASTORS MUST SPEAK THE TRUTH EVEN WHEN IT'S TOUGH

If the preceding points cover material that pastors haven't yet handled, the moment to start teaching and preaching is *now*. There is not a moment to waste. Pastors may have avoided preaching on divorce because they had divorced people in their midst. Pastors may have skirted teaching on the family because their own family wasn't perfect. Pastors might have avoided the issue of homosexuality because they were confused about the origin of this sin.

If this was the case, now is the time for clear words and biblical convictions. The culture is on fire. People are entering our congregations without the slightest shred of a Christian worldview. They don't need stories and jokes. They need the water of life. But this doesn't *only* mean unfolding the means of conversion. It also means preaching and teaching about the tough stuff, the contested ground. It means, like the prophet Jeremiah, saying the hard words, whether people wish to hear them or not.

All God's Word is true; all God's truth is good. Speak the truth even when it's tough for people to receive it. In a joyful, fearless style, drench your people in living water. Preach it from the pulpit. Hold seminars and equipping sessions. If you have Sunday School, do a four-month series on marriage and sexuality. Lead the youth group through a series on manhood and womanhood, singleness and marriage. If you've held back the Bible from speaking to these matters, unmuzzle it. You don't need to shout or grow angry. Whatever your homiletical style, help your people. Don't leave them without God's sure guidance.

There's nothing else to preach. There's nowhere else to go. There's no other God who can save. The Bible is our authority, and the gospel is our hope. If we want to build a marriage culture, we can do no better than to go to the sourcebook of marriage. We should show the people of God, and all who listen in, that the Bible begins with the marriage of a man and a woman and ends with the marriage of a divine groom and his blood-bought bride (Gen. 2; Rev. 21).

This vision of marriage may seem injurious, prejudicially limiting, to a secular culture. But to those who have eyes to see, the union of Christ and his church is nothing less than the hope of mankind. Can we build a marriage culture? The answer depends: will we teach our people these spectacular truths?

4
HUSBANDS, HONOR YOUR WIVES

Greg Gibson

Part of rebuilding a marriage culture in the ruins means pointing the magnifying glass to ourselves as husbands. One giant, counter-cultural way that marriages can be built up in Christ is for husbands to *honor* their wives. What does it mean for a husband to elevate his wife to a place of honor?

FIRST, HONOR YOUR WIFE AS THE WEAKER VESSEL

So often, we talk about women respecting their husbands (Eph. 5:33), which we should, but a gospel-centered, complementarian marriage puts a ginormous spotlight on how men show honor to women. A verse that often gets cracked down on is the unpopular 1 Peter 3:7, which reads, "Likewise, husbands, live with your wives in an understanding way, showing *honor to the woman as the weaker vessel*, since they are heirs with you of the grace of life, so that your prayers may not be hindered" (emphasis mine). It seems Peter is giving specific application for how roles are to be applied within marriage. Peter calls men to live with their wives in an understanding way by showing *honor to her as the weaker vessel.*

What does this mean, though? Weaker vessel, in this context, means of great value. In other words, men honor your wives because they are in a place of high esteem. They are the fine china, not the plastic cups. Men, think about your most important possession and how you treat and honor it. Now triple your efforts and apply that same carefulness in how you treat and honor your wife.

SECOND, HONOR YOUR WIFE BY YOUR GENTLENESS

When we, as men, walk in the Spirit, we can walk with a spirit of gentleness (Gal. 5:22-23). In marriage, men are leaders, providers, and protectors. Out in the world, men are dominion-takers. On the battlefield, men are warriors. But in the home, men are called to be gentle. In fact, in all of life, mature manhood is the pursuit of a courageous gentleness. A posture that says, "I'm a lion, but I'm tame." It is with the same posture that men should pursue their wives.

Paul commands men to pursue gentleness, humility, and mature manhood–the fullness of

Christ (Eph. 4). In your marriage, this means that you are gentle in how you treat your wife, how you talk to your wife, and how you touch your wife. Remember, she is the weaker vessel–an object of intense value. When you pursue Christ first, and allow the fruit of the Spirt to come alive in your heart, then you are able to clothe yourself with gentleness as a man. Only in Christ can you become a tame lion.

THIRD, HONOR YOUR WIFE BY PUTTING HER FIRST IN ALL THINGS

I have conversations often with husbands and wives that are attempting to go 50/50 in their marriages. The husband gives 50%. The wife gives 50%. In this view of marriage, we see marriage as contract. There are no roles. Both parties do all things. We must see marriage, first of all, as a covenant created by God for his glory and given to us for our good (Gen. 1-2; Eph 5). Then, secondly, we live accordingly to how he designed men and women to live within this framework of marriage. If we understand marriage as a covenant, then we come to realize we must both go 100%–not 50/50. And going 100% "all in" means we go "all in" concerning God's design for men and women within marriage.

This also means we go 100% at putting our wife above us. As men, we are second. This is biblical leadership. Practically, this means you honor your wife by putting her in first place. It means you plan around her and the kids. It means date night is stuff she likes to do. It means vacation is to places she wants to go. It means less hobbies for you, less time with your favorite sport or team, and more time (quality and quantity) with her. This is what honoring her means. It means that she is first place. Everything else is last place compared to her.

It means waking up before she does and praying for her and your children. It means spending money on her. Lavishing her with goods and services. It means pursuing her sexually, making her feel as if she is the esteemed and highly valued object of your affections. And it means so many other things, as well. When we pursue and honor our brides in this way, marriage wins.

CONCLUSION

I recently read that leadership is 10% process and 90% building culture. Men should take great counsel in these statistics. Process is the easy part for most of us. Building culture is the difficult part. However, when men clothe themselves in Christ and triple their efforts to build a marriage culture in their homes that is counter-cultural and God-honoring, the world will notice.

It will notice your posture of gentleness and honor towards your wife. It will notice how you put her first in all things. And it will notice the spotlight you place on our great King. Let us work as hard as we possibly can, as tamed lions, to

Husbands, Honor Your Wives

honor our wives as we honor the Lord Jesus Christ.

5
WIVES, SERVE YOUR HUSBANDS
Courtney Reissig

I've never been super creative, or good at baking, or particularly good at ironing. I lack a certain attention to detail for ironing and baking, and all my creative juices are wrapped up in writing, so there isn't much left for crafting or imagining how a room should be organized or decorated (though I wish I had those skills). When I first got married, I thought being a good wife meant all of these things (and a whole host of others). I thought I needed to make elaborate meals from scratch, yet failed to see that we were living on a seminary student budget. I thought I needed to do everything for my husband, yet I didn't understand why he was better served by me taking the time to talk through his theology paper with him. I thought serving my husband meant looking like the wife in my Sunday school class, rather than knowing the man sitting across from me at dinner every night.

I had a lot to learn.

As I look back on my days of misplaced expectations and unhelpful comparison I can't help but think about Jesus' words to Peter when he rebuked him for asking what would happen to John in John 21:20-22. Jesus replied "What is that to you? You follow me."

Isn't that how we so often are when it comes to all manner of things, including how we serve our husbands? We see the wife who irons her husband's shirts every day and wonder if we should be doing the same thing. We hear a wife talk about the notes she leaves for her husband when he travels and assume that we must also prepare notes for our husband when he is away. We measure our competency as a wife by the woman standing next to us and feel the weight of not measuring up.

A SUITABLE HELPER

But this type of thinking fails to understand what God intended when he created Eve to be a helper to Adam, and us a helper to our husbands. She met a need in Adam's life. She was created to serve him uniquely as a helper "fit for him" (Gen 2:18). This also is your role as a wife. When God joined you with your husband in marriage he was meeting a need in your husband's life. You were made to complete what was lacking in his life, to help make him into a better man, and to serve him in ways only you can. This means that you can't look at your friend's marriage and count the ways you don't measure up—or are better than her. It's like comparing apples to oranges. Every marriage is different.

WHEN SERVING IS NATURAL AND UNNATURAL

Marriage is hard. Serving another person that you live in close proximity to is never easy. Add to that the fact that the feelings you have for this other person are intensified by living a full life together with children, a career, ministry, and other obligations, and there is a lot on the table when you daily lay your life down for your husband. Some of the ways you serve him are out of your unique gifting given by God. It comes naturally to you. But then there are ways you are called upon to serve him that are harder. These ways don't come naturally to you. In these moments it is an opportunity for you to count him as more significant than yourself (Phil. 2:3). Marriage is a lesson in humility. It is daily looking to his interests (Phil. 2:4). In all of the ways you serve your husband, both natural and unnatural, you are given a chance to live like Christ, who took on the form of a servant to redeem us and make us his own (Phil 2:5-8).

GETTING PRACTICAL

So, how do you serve your husband? Because every marriage is different and every spouse is different, the answer is actually much simpler than you might think.

Building a Marriage Culture

First, know who you are. The only way you will know what gifts you possess uniquely and what comes naturally to you is if you know who God has created you to be. How has he gifted you? Know these ways and ask him to give you greater insight into how you can cultivate these gifts for the good of others, including your husband.

Second, know your husband. This is where you will see some of the unnatural ways that you are called to serve your husband. Maybe he likes to have things clean and orderly and you don't know the first thing about keeping anything clean and organized. That's a good thing to know about your husband. Marriage is as much about sanctifying us as it is anything else. It is in these moments of knowing your husband (and in turn knowing the ways you may not be like him) that you can see God making you (and him) into new creations that are better together than apart.

Third, look straight ahead to the Savior. Peter's problem was that he was looking away from Jesus and at John's life. My problem was that I was looking away from Christ and at the women around me. He has given me everything I need to accomplish the good works he has prepared for me, including serving my husband (Eph. 2:10). It's not about what the woman next door is doing. It's about what the man sitting next to me in this partnership for life needs most.

6
WOMEN, ESTEEM GODLY MEN

Amanda Peacock

Our 22-year-old son recently graduated college, entered full-time work, found a place to live, and got engaged! It's been a time of celebration and reflection on God's amazing grace. Though I feel sad at our son permanently leaving home, I am reminded in Genesis 2:24 that this is good, and right.

God's design is that men and women fit together not just physically but spiritually and relationally. Both sexes uniquely display different aspects of God's glory. This is explicitly seen when a man and woman marry and portray Christ and the Church.

Men need godly, masculine role models to help them grow in maturity. But women also have a significant role to play. God's purpose for women is to adorn the gospel by their femininity. One of the ways we do this is by esteeming godly masculinity.

FEMININE WOMEN ESTEEM GOD FIRST

True esteem for men will grow out of a heart disposed toward God and not selfish ambition. The heart and mind work in tandem to effect change in the way we think, speak, and act.

A feminine woman does not need a man to complete her because Christ does. He is her Bridegroom above all others. With confidence in Christ she does not need to grasp at equality or compete with men.

Like Sarah, her hope is not ultimately in a man but in God (1 Pt. 3: 5). In Proverbs 31, we see that a biblical woman's greatest characteristic is her fear of God, which means she knows His Word. And it is her pleasure and satisfaction to conscientiously work out her womanhood in obedience to that Word.

FEMININE WOMEN ESTEEM GOD'S DESIGN

A woman who esteems God will also esteem his design for manhood and womanhood.

John Piper says: "At the heart of mature femininity is a freeing disposition to affirm, receive and nurture strength and leadership from worthy men in ways appropriate to a woman's differing relationships."

Here are some women who demonstrate their femininity by esteeming masculinity:

- **Abigail is an example of feminine wisdom and humility.**

Her bold yet non-directive persuasion saved her family from death, and David from the burden of bloodshed (1 Sam. 25).

Abigail demonstrates how esteem for appropriate masculine authority draws out better leadership in a man.

- **Sarah displays what a respectful attitude towards a husband looks like (Gen. 18:12 and 1 Pt. 3:6).**

She was alone in her tent when she referred to Abraham as 'lord'. Sarah wasn't just outwardly obedient to her husband but reverenced him from her heart.

Some wives can say and do the right things but inside they chafe against their husband's leadership, but when a wife esteems God's design in marriage, she will esteem her husband from the inside out. Such a woman looks to cultivate inner beauty over outward adornment. Her disposition is to esteem and be a helper to her husband. A wife can cultivate respect for her husband by being prayerfully thankful to God for giving her a spiritual leader.

- **Esteeming men is not about boosting their egos but about honoring God.**

In fear of the Lord, Esther exercised humility and discretion in speech with Mordecai and the king (Es. 2). In her differing relationships with men she exhibited remarkable self-control.

Esther is a reminder that we ought to choose our words carefully according to the situation and relationship (Eph. 4: 29). A woman like Esther listens well and doesn't constantly interrupt the conversation. Her counsel is winsome and non-directive. Her gentle words build men up.

- **In extraordinary times God uses extra-ordinary means and Deborah is a case in point.**

She respected Barak's role as God's chosen leader and used her influence to encourage him to trust God, and assume his responsibilities (Jdg. 4: 4- 5:12).

A woman like Deborah, who esteems God's design for manhood, can draw out appropriate masculine leadership in the home, or even the workplace where a woman might have a position of authority over men. Biblical femininity can soften even the hardest of hearts (1 Pt. 3: 1-2).

FEMININE WOMEN ESTEEM MASCULINE MEN

Finally, feminine women should esteem and encourage masculine manhood.

Here's John Piper on what this looks like: "At the heart of mature masculinity is a sense of benevolent responsibility to lead, provide for and protect women in ways appropriate to a man's differing relationships."

A true man is a man of the Word and prayer. A man like this is worthy of trust. He has a plan and will commit to doing the hard thing. He will be the one assuming responsibility for those in his care, especially women. Competency isn't the issue, manly character is. A masculine man generally initiates but shows sensitivity to your preferences. He is not prone to self-pity, or self-centeredness but embraces sacrificial leadership, caring for the spiritual and physical welfare of others. He is also a man who submits well to his church elders. This shows humility; good leaders can be led.

A man who is consumed with God and his purposes is a masculine man, and will win a feminine woman's esteem.

Masculinity and femininity has been redeemed in Christ. So at the heart of biblical femininity is the desire for the glory of the gospel to be seen in his design for women, but also men. Complementarity means that women should not compete with men, but rejoice in the beauty of masculinity instead. Therefore, women who esteem God also esteem His design and will gladly esteem godly men.

7
MOTHERS, LOVE YOUR CHILDREN
GraceAnna Castleberry

I was trying desperately to get out the door. The clean dishes were unloaded from the dishwasher and replaced by the sticky ones from breakfast. Oatmeal that was stubbornly clinging to the carpet that had been scrubbed clean. I wiped cheerios and spilled milk off a high chair tray and dashed to the bathroom to apply two minutes worth of make-up and throw my hair in a ponytail.

I picked up two little people one by one, wiped down their sticky hands and faces, changed their diapers, and put on their outfits. While searching frantically for a matching pair of shoes, as if on cue, breakfast hit their tiny tummies. I undressed them, changed their diapers, and redressed them. The lost shoe was found in a toy bin. As I packed the diaper bag, I turned to find my oldest curiously digging through a bag of trash. I moved the trash, took her hand, and started loading both of the girls in

Building a Marriage Culture

the car.

I went around to one car seat, *click, click, click.* And then around to the other, *click, click, click.* I went back inside, grabbed my purse, and took a final look around the house. As hard as I had tried to leave everything clean, it was still messy.

With everyone now loaded up, I got in the car and immediately a voice in the backseat cried for "lovey" which was most certainly left inside.

I looked at the time. *Fifteen minutes late.*

I glanced at the two sweet faces in the back seat, one who was crying. *Should I even try to go where I was headed?* Maybe I should just go back inside. It would be naptime before long.

I closed my eyes and leaned my head against the headrest. *Why couldn't I get it together?*

Why did I feel so frustrated and stressed on a mundane Tuesday?

At that moment a nugget of truth someone once shared with me found it's way into my anxious heart: *"GraceAnna, God has not called you to be the perfect mother. He has called you to be faithful."*

In our Instagram and Pinterest-perfect culture, sometimes it is easy to start comparing ourselves to other women and wondering how they do all the things they do so beautifully.

Whether it is the image of a mom reading books with her little ones on the couch in a magazine worthy home or the many links she may share of the latest craft projects she

Mothers, Love Your Children

completed with her child, feelings of inadequacy can creep into our mothering minds rather quickly.

And we hate those feelings because deep down we really want to be the perfect mom who has it all together. Don't we?

As I grow as a mom, the more I am realizing that feeling inadequate is not always the enemy.

Because anything that causes me to run to the Lord for help can become a good thing.

I'm not the perfect mom. I do struggle and feel frustrated and stressed. And while I should never compare myself to others, I am incredibly inadequate for this momentous task of *raising people.*

We all are.

But if we know Christ, have access to the faithful and perfect one. And he is there *all day long.*

Whether I'm scrubbing spilled milk out of the carpet, searching for a lost shoe, or just feeling stressed and overwhelmed, he is my adequacy.

And he is not so concerned about vacuumed floors or a color coded closet (if someone out there has one of those), he looks at my heart.

> For the LORD sees not as man sees: man looks on the outward appearance, but the LORD looks on the heart" (1 Sam. 16:7).

God doesn't call you to be perfect, *but he is calling to you.*

He is calling you to look to him (Matt. 22:37-39).

He wants you to love your husband and children with the unique gifts and strengths he has *given you*.

And while you will never do these things perfectly, you have a faithful God who will grow you as you try.

"When all around my soul gives way, He then is all my hope and stay."

When things aren't the way you want them to be young mother, run to the faithful one, and find your perfect acceptance in him.

8
WOMEN, OWN YOUR IDENTITY
Candi Finch

Dr. Martin Luther King, Jr. once proclaimed that the ultimate measure of a person is not where he stands in moments of comfort and convenience, but where he stands at times of challenge and controversy. Ladies, we are facing a time of great challenge and controversy in our world today when many people—Christians and non-Christians alike—are rejecting God's standards for living.

For each woman—whether you are married or single, a young woman or a senior saint—you have a vital role to play in God's plan. It is ever more important that we own our God-created identity, not redefine, reinvent, or reimagine it. Despite what our nation or any particular worldview may say, we must remember three key truths.

YOU ARE THE CREATED, NOT THE CREATOR

You are not an accident, nor just some random fluke of some evolutionary process. You have a Creator. He formed you in your mother's womb. That very fact should have significant implications for each of us on a daily basis.

Think about it this way, if you were putting together a bookshelf from Target or Ikea, I hope you would follow the directions provided by the manufacturer (I am still haunted by one failed attempt to go my own way with a Target bookshelf a few years ago!). In the same way, we have a Maker who has given us instructions for how we live life. He says our identity and worth is not grounded in how we look, our marital status, our socio-economic bracket, or even how many likes we get on Facebook or Instagram.

The truth is that we are all sinners. I am and so are you. Our "sin lists" may look different, but Christ died for you and for me. Because of that, you and I and any person who accepts Christ can have a restored relationship with God. That is what our identity should be founded upon.

YOUR SEXUALITY ISN'T ULTIMATELY ABOUT YOU

Our society is in a state of gender neutrality and confusion. My head spins and my heart grieves when I think about how people choose to identify themselves in regards to their sexuality. Facebook alone gives you over fifty "other" choices for gender options other than male or female and will even let you fill in the blank if your "identity" isn't listed. We have really made a mess of God's design and have made it so complicated!

God created men and women as distinct, yet complementary beings (Gen. 1:27, 2:18). While both girls and guys are created in the image of God (Gen. 1:27), God had a specific purpose in mind when He created Eve—she was to be a "helper" for Adam (Gen. 2:18, 20). Being a helper does not mean that Eve was inferior to Adam in any way, but she was distinct from him. Men and women need each other, and this truth about the importance of community was part of God's plan from the beginning of creation (Gen. 2:18).

Why would God create two distinct sexes anyway? One reason is that the way a husband and wife interact with each other should be a picture of the way God interacts with the church (Eph. 5:32). Christian marriages are to be a witness to lost people about the way Christ (pictured through husbands) loves the church (pictured through wives)! Our sexuality was designed to portray/proclaim the very heart and character of God. Even single women portray God's glory by embracing their design as a woman (distinct from man), rather than caving to cultural pressure to define themselves.

YOU ARE CALLED TO BE A LIVING WITNESS OF THE GOODNESS GOD'S PLAN

Probably one of my favorite authors of all time is Jane Austen. In her book, *Mansfield Park*, Austen remarks, "It will, I believe, be everywhere found, that as the clergy are, or are not what they ought to be, so are the rest of the nation."

If we could expand that sentiment to include all Christians and not just clergy, I think it is a chilling reminder of our call to be salt and light. I am afraid the reason so many people are rejecting God's plan is that far too many who claim the name of Christ live lives that mock or discount His plan. Does the way you live life point others to Christ? Are you kind even when you disagree with others? Do you share God's love with respect, knowing that every person is created in the image of God?

We have a great opportunity to share the love of God because of what is happening in our country. We can stand for truth, but we must do so in a way that honors Christ. We must be bold for truth yet kind to those who disagree. We must have courage in the face of opposition and compassion for those who do not yet see the truth of God's plan. The way in which we witness can have an impact on whether or not people want to listen to us.

In Westminster Abbey in London, there is a monument to the English abolitionist William Wilberforce that says many great things about his accomplishments. However, my favorite line from the tribute says, "In an age and country fertile in great and good men, *he was among the foremost of those who fixed the character of their times*; because to high and various talents, to warm benevolence, and to universal candor, he added the abiding eloquence of a Christian life."

Sisters, be women of God who help fix the character of our times. Portray the abiding eloquence of a truly Christian life. As you live day by day, though we may be tempted to wring our hands because of the direction of the culture, we must not lose heart! God is still on His throne. Our mission has not changed. Our call in these times is to "be steadfast, immovable, always abounding in the work of the Lord" (1 Cor. 15:58).

PART 2
RESPONDING TO THE SCOTUS DECISION

9
OFFICIAL RESPONSE TO THE SCOTUS RULING
CBMW Staff & Board

The U. S. Supreme Court's decision in Obergefell v. Hodges tragically continues the culture's shift away from biblical wisdom. As the board and leadership of The Council on Biblical Manhood and Womanhood, we are not moving an inch from our fundamental commitments to biblical marriage, to manhood and womanhood, and to the God-created natural family.

We recognize the following truths as grounded in the Word of God and given for God's glory and our joy.

1. BIBLICAL MARRIAGE IS DEFINED AS A COVENANT RELATIONSHIP BETWEEN ONE MAN AND ONE WOMAN (GEN. 1:26-27; 2:24; MATT. 19:4-6; EPH. 5:21-33; COL. 3:18-19)

Biblical marriage between a man and a woman is the design of Almighty God. It is a central means to flourishing and the initiator of the first institution, the natural family. It is a vital part of our churches and our communities. When the biblical definition of marriage is compromised, the very foundation of society is radically compromised, and children will suffer.

2. SEXUAL COMPLEMENTARITY UNDERGIRDS BIBLICAL MARRIAGE (GEN. 1:28, 2:18, 21-24; 1 COR. 11:7-9; 1 TIM. 2:12-14)

God designed human sexuality for a purpose. The distinct but complementary realities of manhood and womanhood are ordained by God and foundational to the created order. The sexual complementarity of equal image-bearers—husband and wife—brings pleasure to the couple, allows for the bearing and rearing of children, and helps fulfill the dominion mandate. God created the husband to be the "head" of his family and the wife to be his "helper."

3. BIBLICAL MARRIAGE PICTURES THE GOSPEL OF JESUS CHRIST (EPH. 5:21-33)

The sacrificial love of the husband for his wife and the wife's loving submission to her husband illumines Christ's love and sacrificial death for his church. If the church compromises the Bible's

Official Response to the SCOTUS Ruling

teaching on biblical marriage, the church misconstrues the gospel itself. This structure alone displays the uniqueness and beauty of biblical marriage.

4. HOMOSEXUALITY IS DECLARED BY GOD A SIN (LEV. 18:22; DEUT. 23:17-18; ROM. 1:26-27; 1 COR. 6:9; 1 TIM. 1:10)

Homosexuality not only is a violation of the natural order, but is a violation of the moral will and law of God. Without repentance and faith in Christ, all those persisting in any sin, including the sin of homosexuality, will be judged on the last day by Jesus Christ.

5. THE TRUE CHURCH OF JESUS CHRIST WILL NOT CAVE ON BIBLICAL MARRIAGE (2 COR. 4:2; EPH. 5:21-33; 2 JN. 9; JUDE 3)

Since the true church of Jesus Christ stands or falls on the gospel of Jesus Christ and because biblical marriage is so clearly defined in Scripture, faithfulness to the Word of God on the truth of biblical marriage is a mark of the true church of Jesus Christ. To depart from the faith once for all delivered to the saints on this issue is to depart from Christ Himself.

6. WE WILL CONTINUE TO LOVE AND EXTEND GRACE TO EVERY SINNER (MATT. 5:14; LUKE 14:23; ROM. 3:23; 1 COR. 5:12; EPH. 2:8-9)

As the church of Jesus Christ, sinners made perverse by the fall of Adam, we will love and extend the grace of God to all people without exception. Because any sin of any kind separates us from a holy and righteous God, we will strive to be "the light of the world" and a "city on a hill," holding forth the only remedy for reconciliation with God to a world that is lost, broken, and in desperate need of grace.

It is the solemn and sacred commitment of CBMW to promote these truths and defend them from compromise. We are unfazed by the culture's challenges and brimming with confidence in the power of the Word to save and restore fallen humanity. The gospel was not made for the high places, but for the shadowlands.

In 2015, in light of the Obergefell ruling, we gladly reaffirm the Danvers Statement. We call churches across the geographical and denominational spectrum to stand with us in promoting a biblical vision of marriage through both proclamation and action. This we will do by preaching the truth about manhood, womanhood, and the family, by creating strong marriage cultures and families in our churches, and by lovingly calling every sinner to the grace of repentance and the glad way of holiness.

Official Response to the SCOTUS Ruling

—

Owen Strachan (President)

Grant Castleberry (Executive Director)

K. Erik Thoennes (Chairman of the Board)

J. Ligon Duncan (Board Member)

Daniel L. Akin (Board Member)

Jason Duesing (Board Member)

Wayne Grudem (Board Member)

Jeff Purswell (Board Member)

Thomas White (Board Member)

10
THE SUPREME COURT HAS RULED: WHAT SHOULD CHRISTIANS DO?

Owen Strachan

Same-sex marriage is now legal in all 50 states, per the ruling in Obergefell v. Hodges. What should Christians think and do in response?

1. WE SHOULD RECOGNIZE THAT THIS IS A DARK HOUR FOR AMERICA

This development has not occurred in a vacuum. It is the realization of many decades of cultural decline. Our country's identity has symbolically shifted from a Judeo-Christian nation to a neo-pagan one.

2. THE ENLIGHTENMENT HAS PRESENTLY OVERWHELMED THE GREAT AWAKENING

We have embraced a vision of sexuality and humanity that has nothing to do with biblical truth and traditional wisdom. A secular view of mankind scrubbed of religious ideals and driven by vague notions of "equality" has triumphed over the religious understanding of mankind as a created being responsible to obey and worship the Creator.

3. ADULTS HAVE CHOSEN TO CATER TO THEMSELVES RATHER THAN TO CHILDREN

Marriage–the covenantal union of a man and a woman–blesses spouses. But it also serves to protect and care for children. Children need a father and a mother. With this ruling, we will now witness many children growing up in compromised homes. This development will cause real suffering in the lives of little boys and girls.

4. RIGHTS NOW TAKE PRECEDENCE OVER DUTIES IN AMERICA

Our self-obsessed society has made good on its orientation. We now care more about personal rights, rights which have no constitutional precedent, than we do about duties to God, family, country, and community.

5. THE CHURCH IS NOW A MARGINALIZED COMMUNITY

Our witness has not carried the day in the public square. To a considerable degree, we now find ourselves at the mercy of those who disagree with us.

****

So what should we do?

WE SHOULD DO EXACTLY WHAT WE HAVE BEEN DOING

God is reigning now as he was before this ruling. Our lives are not determined by rulers of this world. They are shaped by the decrees of a greater ruler.

WE SHOULD PRAY

We should ask the Lord to do a mighty work amidst the wreckage of this decision, to convert sinners, to rouse the church to moral witness, and to do mighty and unthinkable things in our time. We should petition God to grant us favor such that our churches and organizations will continue to flourish.

WE SHOULD INVEST IN THE CHURCH

More than we've likely ever felt, our congregations are little outposts of the kingdom.

We should help build our local churches and make clear to all we can that they are way-stations of grace in the name of Jesus Christ. We now have a terrific opportunity to show people drawn to homosexuality that we really do love them, and that we are ready more than ever to receive them into membership through repentance and faith. We may be beaten in the broader culture at present, but we're not keeping score. We're not in this, ultimately, to win political victories (important as they are), but to minister grace and truth. We are thrilled to have the opportunity to do just that.

WE SHOULD PLUNGE BACK INTO THE PUBLIC SQUARE

This is a Supreme Court ruling. It's a very big deal. But it's only the latest such major event. We've seen slavery struck down in America; we've witnessed the long, slow death of Jim Crow in the twentieth-century. Christians of all people believe in divine reversals, shocking redemption, and Copernican revolutions. We are the people of hope. We've seen Abraham made into a mighty nation, Israel march out of Egypt, mighty Babylon and fierce Persia and lordly Rome crumble into ash, the church explode as the gospel slipped its first-century cage. We believe in a God of ridiculous power who does inconceivable things. From this backdrop, we are poised to plunge back into the public square out of love for neighbor and the pursuit of shalom for all people, including those who oppose us.

LASTLY, WE SHOULD CULTIVATE OUR FAMILIES AND REINVEST IN OUR MARRIAGES

It's right and even needed to seek the reversal of this decision and the undoing of its many baleful effects. We must and should do that, and every single Christian should participate meaningfully in the political system at every level they can. But let's get this straight: our major work going forward, along with what I've said thus far, should in truth be the cultivation of our own gardens.

Let's allow this decision to shock us back into taking stock of the log in our own eye. Let's use it to motivate us to dig into our marriage and truly love our God-given spouse. Let's recommit to loving our children in a distinctly biblical way. May this Supreme Court decision awaken God's people to display the beauty of complementarity as never before, to put the union of a self-sacrificial head to his loving bride on IMAX display wherever we are.

The church may feel shaken. The culture may seem to be crumbling. But God is on his own throne and his gospel is on the move. America is the new Rome. But Rome is where the message of Christ crucified and resurrected slipped its surly bonds. Rome is where the church flourished and grew despite terrific opposition. Rome tried to snuff out the light of Christ, but in total honesty, Rome failed miserably.

May the church of America be like the church of Rome.

11
PARENTING IN A GAY MARRIAGE WORLD: WHAT SHOULD CHRISTIAN PARENTS DO?

Greg Gibson

As you now know, same-sex marriage is legal in all 50 states. If you have children, they will now grow-up in a culture that recognizes the legitimacy of homosexuality. What should parents do in response?

1. TALK HONESTLY AND OPENLY ABOUT SIN, HOMOSEXUALITY, AND GAY MARRIAGE WITH YOUR CHILDREN

We live in a post-Genesis 3 world. Because of this, sin is a reality, both in our lives and in the lives of our children. Part of the goal of parenting is teaching our children to love God and hate sin. Using your *conscience* as a parent, and discerning the *appropriateness of their age*, talk openly with your children about homosexuality and gay marriage. Unless you live in the mountains, have no technology, and your children have zero friends, I promise they are already chatting about this issue with their friends. Six, seven, and eight-year-olds are already having these conversations in lunch rooms and on school playgrounds. Your children's classmates might have 2 mommies or 2 daddies. Too often, parents want this to be a hush hush issue with their children until later in middle or high school. By then, it's too late. As your conscience, the Holy Spirit, and Lady Wisdom guide you, talk honestly and openly about this issue with your children.

2. MODEL TO YOUR CHILDREN A MARRIAGE THAT IS A PICTURE OF THE GOSPEL

As Owen Strachan put it (President of CBMW), "Let's allow this decision to shock us back into taking stock of the log in our own eye. Let's use it to motivate us to dig into our marriage and truly love our God-given spouse. Let's recommit to loving our children in a distinctly biblical way. May this Supreme Court decision awaken God's people to display the beauty of complementarity as never before, to put the union of a self-sacrificial head to his loving bride on IMAX display wherever we are." As Strachan alludes, the home is the most foundational place for your children to learn the gospel and see it modeled. Let us recommit to pursuing our marriages before anything else. Let us model to our children the entire gospel within our marriages–servant headship, submission, grace, repentance, and restoration.

3. TEACH YOUR CHILDREN THE BIBLICAL FOUNDATIONS FOR MARRIAGE

Teach your children the foundation for marriage from Genesis 1-2, the mysteries of its relationship between Christ and the Church in Ephesians 5, and how marriage ultimately wins when Jesus returns in Revelation 19. Talk about this often with your children. Show your children often pictures and videos from your wedding. Never talk poorly about marriage. Elevate it as the most important pursuit.

4. TEACH YOUR CHILDREN THE BIBLICAL FOUNDATIONS FOR SEX

Many parents are waiting until late in middle school to talk with their children about sex for the first time. Again, in my opinion, this is too late. I would encourage somewhere around 4th, 5th, or 6th grade to truly begin the "sex talk" with your children. A good way to start this conversation is for dads to take sons, and moms to take daughters, on what is called a *purity weekend*. Take your children somewhere fun, do more expensive things (because this weekend should be awesome), and begin the conversation about sex with your children. Notice I said *begin*. This is not a one-time conversation. This needs to be an ongoing discussion with your children.

5. PROTECT YOUR CHILDREN FROM THE INFLUENCES OF PORNOGRAPHY

Like a warrior fighting his enemy on the battle field, may parents fight to protect their children from the influences of pornography! This is not a light task. Some researchers have stated that the average age of first exposure to pornography is down to eight. Eight! I'll repeat, EIGHT! Children can access pornography on any device in the home today (cell phones, television, iPads, computers, gaming systems, and more). What is more, Covenant Eyes is a great filtering software you can put on your devices. Teach your children why this filtering software is on your devices. It's not because you don't trust them (which you shouldn't, though), it's because we want to put guardrails in our lives and completely crush any form of temptation to sin.

6. PRAY FERVENTLY FOR AND WITH YOUR CHILDREN

As the influences of culture creep closer to our doorsteps, let us pray fervently for the hearts and minds of our children. The battle is not against flesh and blood, but against the spiritual forces of this world (Eph. 6:12). Let us pray that God would protect, build up, and send out our children into the world as ambassadors for Him (2 Cor. 5:20).

7. PARTNER WITH A GOSPEL-CENTERED LOCAL CHURCH THAT WILL COME ALONGSIDE YOU AND TEACH THE TRUTHS OF SCRIPTURE

Discipleship primarily happens in the home, but the local church should also be a great resource for equipping and building up your family. So often, parents view the local church as the center of discipleship. It's not. As parents, that is your job. The local church should come alongside of you in teaching your children the truths of Scripture. Here is our growing list of churches that are like-minded in teaching these important truths. If there is not one in your area on the list, let us know, and maybe we can help you find one.

8. TEACH YOUR CHILDREN BIBLICAL GENDER ROLES

As you teach marriage and model marriage to your children, it is important to teach your children biblical gender roles, too. Men are designed by God to be leaders, providers, and protectors in the home. Women are designed by God to be helpers and nurturers in the home. Men and women are equal in dignity, value, and worth, but different in role and function. This is powerhouse complementarianism.

9. TRAIN YOUR CHILDREN TOWARDS COURAGEOUS BIBLICAL MANHOOD AND WOMANHOOD

Being a man who practices the marks of mature biblical manhood is completely counter-cultural–and likewise for women who practice mature biblical womanhood. We are called by God to pass down the truths of manhood and womanhood to the next generation (Titus 2). We pass these truths and characteristics down by teaching and modeling them.

10. DON'T PANIC. TRUST IN GOD. HE IS STILL IN CONTROL. HIS PLAN WILL STILL WIN

The sky is not falling. The world is not going to hell. God is still in control. Let us live with this bold posture. Talk with your children about this issue just like you would about any issue. As Christians, we are "sent into" the world to seek the redemption of the world (Rom. 8) and be instruments used by God in the building of his Church (Matt. 28:16-20). Remember, we are "sent into" the world by our Chief Commander armed with truth & love. We await His triumphant re-entry. For Christians, nothing changes. Same mindset. Same posture. Same mission. Same victorious King. When we understand this, we realize that love (and truth) wins.

ABOUT THE AUTHORS

Owen Strachan is CBMW President and Associate Professor of Christian Theology at Midwestern Baptist Theological Seminary in Kansas City, Missouri. At MBTS, he teaches systematic theology and supervises doctoral students while serving as the Director for the Center on Gospel & Culture. He has authored numerous books and written in academic journals like Themelios, Trinity, & JBMW and in popular publications like The Atlantic and Christianity Today. He speaks regularly for churches and conferences, and has been profiled in World magazine as a young evangelical leader and has been profiled in Baptist Press for his pro-life work. Follow him on Twitter @ostrachan.

Grant Castleberry serves as the Executive Director for CBMW. He is also a PhD student in Historical Theology at the Southern Baptist Theological Seminary. He is a former Captain in the Marine Corps. He holds a B.S. from Texas A&M and an M.Div from The Southern Baptist Theological Seminary. He and his wife, GraceAnna, reside in Frankfurt, Kentucky with their three children. Follow him on Twitter @grcastleberry.

Greg Gibson is a husband, dad, pastor, and writer. He is the Executive Editor at the Council on Biblical Manhood & Womanhood (CBMW), and he is the author of *Date Different: A Short (but real) Conversation on Dating, Sex, and Marriage for Teenagers (and their parents)*. Follow him on Twitter @greggibson86.

Gavin Peacock is married to Amanda and they have two children, Jake and Ava. He is also a pastor at Calvary Grace Church of Calgary and the Director of International Outreach for CBMW. He was born in Kent, England, where he played professional football (insert soccer for N.A. audiences) for 18 years. Gavin was converted to Christ at age 18 and was used by God to bear witness to the gospel through his career. However, in 2006 God called him to full time pastoral ministry. He holds an MACS. Follow him on Twitter @GPeacock8.

GraceAnna is a wife and a mom to three children. She also co-hosts the radio show Mothering from the Heart with her mom, AudreyBroggi, which airs weekly on WAGP. She holds a B.A. in Early Childhood Education from Clemson University. She formerly served on Cru staff at Duke University. She and her husband,

About the Authors

Grant, reside in Frankfort, Kentucky with their three children. Follow her on Twitter @gacastleberry.

Courtney Reissig is a writer, wife, and mom to three boys. She is married to Daniel, and together they live in Little Rock, Arkansas, and serve at Midtown Baptist Church. She is the author of *The Accidental Feminist: Restoring Our Delight in God's Good Design* (Crossway, 2015). Follow her on Twitter @courtneyreissig.

Amanda Peacock is a wife and mother. She and her husband, Gavin, have been married for 26 years. They live in Canmore, Alberta, having moved there seven years ago from the U.K. They are members of Calvary Grace Church, Calgary, where Gavin serves as one of the pastors and Amanda co-teaches the women's ministry. She loves spending time with her family, meeting with young women, practicing hospitality and enjoying the outdoors.

Candi Finch serves as Assistant Professor of Theology in Women's Studies at Southwestern Baptist Theological Seminary in Fort Worth, TX. Her greatest passion is to see teenage girls and women come to know the Lord and become mature disciples of Christ. Candi has contributed to such volumes as the Women's Evangelical Commentary on the New Testament and Old

Testament and also the The Study Bible for Women. You can read more of her writing at www.biblicalwoman.com. Follow her on Twitter @Candi_Finch.